SUPER SIMPLE
FAT QUARTER QUILTS

Lynda Milligan & Nancy Smith

SPECIAL THANKS

Sewing & Quilting – Jane Dumler, Ann Petersen, Courtenay Hughes, Susan Auskaps, Sue Williams, Katie Wells, Kelly Kiel

Long-arm Machine Quilting – Susan Geddes, Carolyn Schmitt, Sandi Fruehling, Kay Morrison

Selected Props – From the homes of our friends at Great American Quilt Factory, and the homes of Susan and Bob Julian and Jacqui Aubertot

BOOK PRODUCTION

Sharon Holmes – Editor, Technical Illustrator

Susan Johnson – Quilt Designer, Illustrator, Photo Stylist

Lexie Foster – Cover Designer, Quilt Designer, Illustrator

Christine Scott – Editorial Assistant

Sandi Fruehling – Copy Reader

Brad Bartholomew – Photographer

Every effort has been made to ensure that the information in this book is accurate. Due to individual skills, conditions, and tools, we cannot be responsible for any losses, injuries, or other damages that may result from its use.

Fabric Designers for AvLyn, Inc. • Publishers of Possibilities® Books

HOME OF GREAT AMERICAN QUILT FACTORY, INC.

FAT QUARTERS

What is a fat quarter? One by itself is a precut piece of fabric 18″ x 21-22″—18″ by half the width of the fabric. When combined by the quilt shop into packets, fat quarters become beautiful, tempting, collectible bundles of color!

What to do with them when we get them home? Easy! Choose a quilt in this book and dive in!

Our two previous *super simple* books, **Super Simple Squares** and **Super Simple Strips**, are based on, but not dependent on, precut bundles or packets of fabrics. **Super Simple Fat Quarter Quilts** is based on groups of individually chosen fat quarters, but purchased yardage or fabrics pulled from your stash will also work. The only parameter is to have eight (or sixteen) pieces at least 18″ x 21-22″ (18″ by half the width of the fabric). Our cutting plans use 17″ x 20″ of each fat quarter.

We do not recommend prewashing fat quarters.
Shrinkage may not leave enough usable fabric.

IMPORTANT DIAGRAMS

For each quilt, we have included detailed cutting diagrams. It is important to understand these diagrams before beginning to cut since there is very little margin for error.

QUILT CATEGORIES

There are several categories of quilts in this book based on the way they are made and the design elements they contain.

SIMPLE SQUARES & RECTANGLES - *Ashley*, page 10, is a very simple quilt made of two sizes of squares and one size of rectangle. It would make a perfect first project for the beginning quilter. The same is true of **Hyde Park**, page 6, which has a simple rectangle of a beautiful print for the center and is surrounded by a border of plain squares cut from the fat quarters.

SLASHED - Two of our designs are made by "slashing" the four 8½″ squares you get from each fat quarter. *Butterfly Kisses*, page 12, uses the slashing technique to make soft, varied background squares over which applique is stitched. *Confetti*, page 14, is made of squares that are slashed to get center triangles. Trading the center triangles with the backgrounds cut from other slashed squares results in many color combinations and lots of fun!

HALF-SQUARE TRIANGLES - Many of the quilts have half-square triangle units. Following are two different methods for the accurate cutting and stitching of these units.

HALF-SQUARE TRIANGLE UNITS
METHOD 1 - PHOTOCOPY OUR TRIANGLE GRIDS
• Page 43 - 2″-finished half-square triangle units
• Page 44 - 2½″-finished half-square triangle units
• Page 45 - 3″-finished half-square triangle units

Photocopy the required number of pages of triangle grids for your quilt on a copier that reproduces at an accurate 100%. Check first copy before making others. Choose a lightweight paper that tears away easily such as paper made especially for foundation piecing.

Tape copies together, matching solid lines, to make the configuration in the cutting diagram for your quilt. Place the two fabrics for the units *right sides together* with the lighter fabric on top, then place the triangle paper on top of the lighter fabric. *Stitch on the dotted lines* using a short machine stitch (15 per inch). *Cut on the solid lines* using a rotary cutter and ruler. Gently press the triangle units open with the seam allowances toward the darker fabric. Carefully tear off paper.

Example with 3″-finished triangle grid

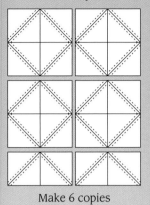

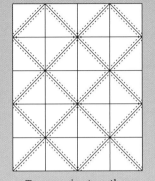

Make 6 copies

Tape copies together
matching solid lines

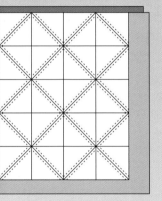

Place fabrics **right
sides together** & place
paper on top

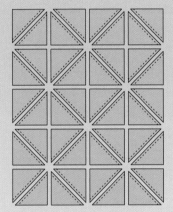

Stitch on dotted lines,
cut on solid lines, press,
tear off paper

Makes
40 units

METHOD 2 - MAKE PAIRS OF UNITS

This method requires no grid or paper and is extremely accurate. It involves cutting squares from layered fabric with a rotary cutter, then making two half-square triangle units from each set. Following the cutting diagram for the quilt you are making, place fabric pieces for triangle units *right sides together*. Cut squares for each pair of triangle units. (2⅞″ squares for 2″-finished units, 3⅜″ squares for 2½″-finished units, 3⅞″ squares for 3″-finished units.) Draw a diagonal line across each set. Stitch ¼″ from each side of drawn diagonal line. Cut each square in half on the diagonal line. Gently press the triangle units with the seam allowances toward the darker fabric.

Example with 3″-finished half-square triangle units

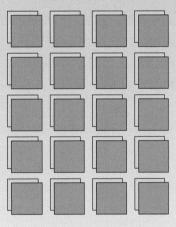

Draw diagonal line
on each set &
stitch ¼″ away

Cut on line

Place fabrics **right sides
together** & cut sets of squares

Each set
makes 2 units

BORDERS - BLUNT CORNER

1. To determine length of side borders, measure length of quilt from cut edge to cut edge in at least three places. Average these measurements. Do not measure along the edges since edges are often stretched and can be longer.

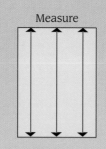

Measure

2. Stitch selvage-to-selvage cuts of fabric end to end, or cut lengthwise pieces as directed, to equal average length of quilt top.

3. Fold one side border and one side of quilt top into quarters and mark with pins. Matching marked points, pin border to quilt, right sides together. This distributes any ease along entire edge of quilt.

Mark & Stitch

4. Stitch border to quilt. If one edge is slightly longer (usually the quilt top), put that side against the feed-dog, and excess will be eased into seam. Repeat for other side of quilt.

5. Repeat measuring and stitching process for top and bottom borders of quilt.

Repeat For Top & Bottom

6. For a second or third border, measure down center of previous border. Stitch side borders to quilt, then measure for top and bottom borders.

7. Press border seams toward outside edge of quilt.

BORDERS - MITERED CORNER
MEASURE AND PREPARE BORDERS

1. To determine length to prepare side borders, measure quilt length without borders as described in Step 1 of blunt corner borders, above. Add to this measurement, double the width of all planned borders of quilt, then add 2-4″ extra (yardage charts include this extra fabric).

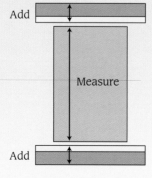

Add

Measure

Add

2. To determine length to prepare the top and bottom borders, measure quilt top width without borders and add double the width of all borders of quilt plus 2-4″ extra.

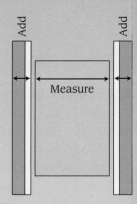

Add

Add

Measure

3. Stitch selvage-to-selvage cuts of fabric together if necessary, to make needed lengths, or cut seamless border strips on lengthwise grain. If quilt has more than one border, sew individual borders for each side together first to make complete border units. Press seam allowances toward outside edge of quilt.

PIN AND STITCH BORDERS TO QUILT

1. Measure length of quilt without borders from seam line to seam line by measuring center of quilt in several places. Do not measure along edge of quilt as it is often stretched and measurement will be longer than a measurement taken across center. Average these measurements.

2. Find center of long inside edge of one side border unit and mark with a pin. Measure from pin each direction one-half the quilt length measurement minus ¼″ and mark with pins. These marks correspond to corner seam intersections.

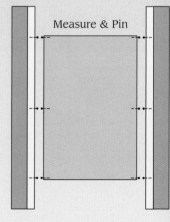

Measure & Pin

3. Find center of quilt side by folding and mark with a pin. Pin side border unit to quilt side, right sides together, matching corner seam intersections on quilt to corresponding marked points on border; match centers. Pin at intervals.

4. Stitch, beginning and ending stitching at corner seam intersections.

5. Repeat for other side, then for top and bottom.

PRESS AND STITCH MITER

1. Lay a corner of quilt, right side up, on ironing board. Quilt may be pinned to ironing board to keep it from falling off or being distorted. With borders overlapping, fold one border under at a 45° angle. Match seams and work with it until it matches perfectly. Outer edges should be square and without fullness. Border seams should create a 90° angle. Press this fold.

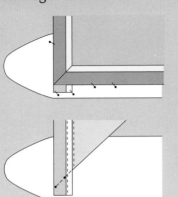

2. Flip outside edge of border with pressed fold over to other outside edge of border, right sides together; pin along pressed fold, placing pins parallel to the fold line. Open and check for accuracy before stitching. Stitch from inner corner to outside of quilt, backstitching at both ends.

3. Lay mitered corner of quilt on ironing board right side up to see if seams match, Press. Trim seam to ¼". Repeat for other three corners.

BINDING - DOUBLE-FOLD, MITERED

1. Trim batting and backing even with quilt top.

2. Cut strips selvage to selvage. Stitch end to end to fit all the way around quilt.

3. Press binding in half lengthwise, wrong sides together. Leaving a 6" tail of binding, begin stitching binding to right side of quilt at least 12" from one corner. Stop stitching at seam intersection of first corner. Leave needle in fabric, pivot, and stitch off corner of quilt.

4. Pull quilt slightly away from machine, leaving threads attached. Make a 45° fold in binding.

5. Fold again, placing second fold even with top edge of quilt and raw edges of binding even with right raw edge of quilt.

6. Resume stitching at top edge.

7. After making all four mitered corners, stop stitching 6" from where you started. Take quilt out of machine. Lay ends of binding along unstitched edge of quilt. Trim ends so they overlap by ½".

8. Unfold binding and pull ends away from quilt. Place ends of binding right sides together, stitch with ¼" seam, and finger press seam open. Refold binding and place it along unstitched edge of quilt. Stitch remaining section of binding to quilt.

9. Turn binding to back and hand stitch folded edge to cover stitched line. To distribute bulk, fold each corner miter in the opposite direction from which it was folded and stitched on the front.

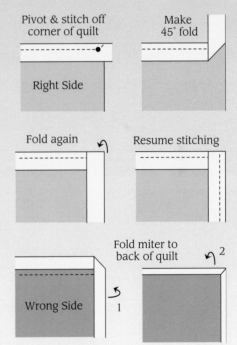

Pivot & stitch off corner of quilt

Make 45° fold

Right Side

Fold again

Resume stitching

Fold miter to back of quilt

Wrong Side

HYDE PARK

56 x 67"

See other colorations for this quilt on page 30.

YARDAGE

Choose fabric with 42" usable width.
We do not recommend prewashing fat quarters.

Border 2	8 fat quarters - 18" x 21-22"
Center	1½ yd
Border 1	½ yd
Binding	⅝ yd
Backing	3¾ yd
Batting	62 x 73"

CUTTING

Cut strips selvage to selvage.

Border 2	See Step 1
Center	1 piece 37¾ x 49"
Border 1	5 strips 2½" wide
Binding	7 strips 2½" wide

DIRECTIONS

Use ¼" seam allowance unless otherwise noted.

1. BORDER 2 CUTTING: Use diagram to cut fat quarters.

Cut from each fat quarter:
16 squares 4¼"

2. BORDER 1: Make 2 side borders by piecing strips to same length as quilt. Stitch to quilt. Press. Cut top and bottom borders to fit quilt. Stitch to quilt. Press. More information in General Directions, page 4.

3. BORDER 2: Stitch squares together in pairs, then stitch pairs together—14 pairs for side borders and 15 pairs for top and bottom borders. Stitch side borders to quilt, then top and bottom borders. Press. See diagram on page 30.

Sides: 14 squares long

Top/Bottom: 15 squares long

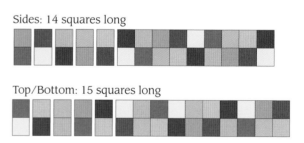

Continued on page 30

SUNNY DAYS

50x61″ 2¾″ squares

NOTE: Make this quilt even more *super simple* by omitting the scallops.

YARDAGE

Choose fabric with 42″ usable width.
We do not recommend prewashing fat quarters.

Center	8 fat quarters - 18″ x 21-22″
Border 1	⅓ yd
Border 2	1⅝ yd
Binding	⅔ yd
Backing	3⅜ yd
Batting	56x67″

CUTTING

Cut strips selvage to selvage.

Center	See Step 1
Border 1	4 strips 2″ wide
Border 2	4 pieces 9½″ wide cut on lengthwise grain
Binding	**bias** strips 1½″ wide
	to equal approx 300″ when stitched end to end

DIRECTIONS

Use ¼″ seam allowance unless otherwise noted.

1. CENTER CUTTING: Use diagram to cut fat quarters.

Cut from each fat quarter:
25 squares 3¼″

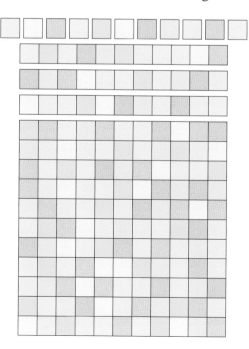

2. ASSEMBLY: Arrange squares in a setting of 11x15 with random placement of fabrics. Stitch into horizontal rows. Stitch rows together. Press.

8

Continued on page 31

ASHLEY

44x60" 8" Block
See other colorations for this quilt on page 32.

YARDAGE

Choose fabric with 42" usable width.
We do not recommend prewashing fat quarters.

Blocks   8 fat quarters - 18" x 21-22"
Border 1   ⅓ yd
Border 2   1⅛ yd
Binding   ⅝ yd
Backing   3 yd
Batting   50x66"

CUTTING

Cut strips selvage to selvage.

Blocks   See Step 1
Border 1   4-5 strips 1½" wide
Border 2   6 strips 5½" wide
Binding   6 strips 2½" wide

DIRECTIONS

Use ¼" seam allowance unless otherwise noted.

1. BLOCK CUTTING: Use diagram to cut fat
   quarters.

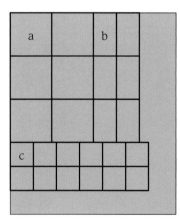

Cut from each
fat quarter:

a - 6 squares 4½"
b - 6 pieces 2½"x4½"
c - 12 squares 2½"

2. BLOCKS: Make 24 blocks using fabrics in
   random positions. Press.

For each block:

Make
2

Make
24

3. ASSEMBLY: Arrange blocks in a 4x6 setting,
   rotating every other block as shown. Stitch into
   horizontal rows. Stitch rows together. Press.

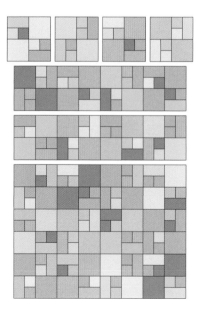

10

Continued on page 32

BUTTERFLY KISSES

54 x 66″   6″ Block
See other colorations for this quilt on page 33.

YARDAGE

Choose fabric with 42″ usable width.
We do not recommend prewashing fat quarters.

Blocks	16 fat quarters - 18″ x 21-22″
Border 1	½ yd
Border 2	1½ yd
Applique	⅛ yd each dark pink, white, bright green
	⅙ yd each medium pink, lavender, purple
	¼ yd dark green - stems, flower leaves
	⅝ yd medium green - flower & plain leaves
Binding	⅝ yd
Backing	3⅝ yd
Batting	60 x 72″
Fusible web	3 yd

CUTTING

Cut strips selvage to selvage.

Blocks	See Step 1
Border 1	8 strips 1½″
Border 2	8 strips 5½″
Applique	patterns on page 47
	5 flowers with 4 leaves each
	2 flowers with 3 leaves each
	50 plain leaves, 50 reversed
	4 butterflies
	stems - see Step 4
Binding	7 strips 2½″ wide

DIRECTIONS

Use ¼″ seam allowance unless otherwise noted.

1. BLOCK CUTTING: Use diagrams to cut fat quarters. Mark and make cuts as shown without moving pieces out of their general position.

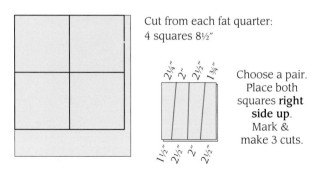

Cut from each fat quarter:
4 squares 8½″

Choose a pair. Place both squares **right side up**. Mark & make 3 cuts.

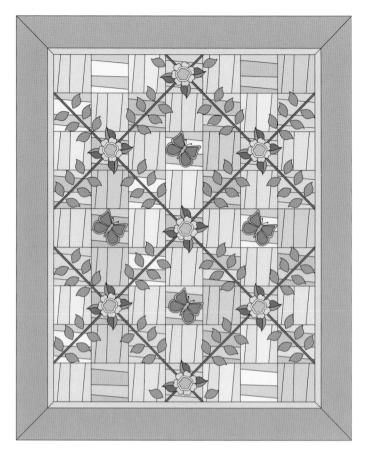

2. BLOCKS: Swap pieces as shown to make 2 blocks. Stitch. Press. Trim each to 6½″ square. Make 63.

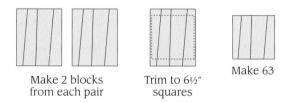

Make 2 blocks from each pair   Trim to 6½″ squares   Make 63

3. ASSEMBLY: Arrange blocks in a 7x9 setting, rotating as shown on page 33. Stitch into horizontal rows. Stitch rows together. Press.

4. APPLIQUE: For stems, fuse web to wrong side of 3x42″ piece of dark green fabric. Cut seven ¼″ x 42″ strips. Place flowers (with their leaves) in centers of blocks as shown on whole-quilt diagram above. Slide stems under flowers, trimming as needed to hide raw ends. Stems

Continued on page 33

CONFETTI

42 x 54"   6" Block
See other colorations for this quilt on page 34.

YARDAGE

Choose fabric with 42" usable width.
We do not recommend prewashing fat quarters.

Blocks	16 fat quarters - 18" x 21-22"
Binding	⅝ yd
Backing	3 yd
Batting	48 x 60"

CUTTING

Cut strips selvage to selvage.

Blocks	See Step 1
Binding	6 strips 2½" wide

DIRECTIONS

Use ¼" seam allowance unless otherwise noted.

1. BLOCK CUTTING: Use diagrams to cut fat quarters. Stack squares in sets of 4 or 8, all pieces **right side up** (choose to cut either 4 or 8 layers depending on the sharpness of your rotary cutter blade). Mark and make cuts as shown without moving pieces out of their general position.

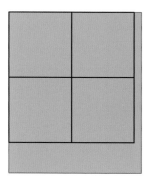

Cut from each
fat quarter:
4 squares 8½"

Mark   1st Cut

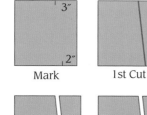

Mark   2nd Cut

Mark   3rd Cut

Keep pieces
in position
while sewing
blocks

2. BLOCKS: As you sew the blocks, choose centers to contrast with the backgrounds. Stitch background pieces to center triangle in order shown. Press. Trim each block to 6½" square. Rotary rulers come in this size and make this step very easy. Ruler can be tilted and moved around slightly on the block for more variety in the finished blocks. Make 63.

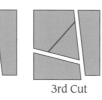

Choose centers
as you sew

Centered &
stitched

Continued on page 34

14

SAFARI

52 x 67"   6" Block
See other colorations for this quilt on page 35.

YARDAGE

Choose fabric with 42" usable width.
We do not recommend prewashing fat quarters.

Blocks	8 fat quarters - 18" x 21-22"
	4 lights, 4 darks
Sashing	1 yd - rectangles
	¼ yd - squares
Border 1	¼ yd
Border 2	1½ yd
Binding	⅝ yd
Backing	3½ yd
Batting	58 x 73"

CUTTING

Cut strips selvage to selvage.

Blocks	See Step 1
Sashing	82 rectangles 2 x 6½"
	48 squares 2"
Border 1	5 strips 1" wide
Border 2	6-7 strips 6½" wide
Binding	6-7 strips 2½" wide

DIRECTIONS

Use ¼" seam allowance unless otherwise noted.

1. BLOCK CUTTING: Choose a method of cutting and sewing half-square triangle units from General Directions, pages 2-3. This quilt requires 3"-finished triangle units. (If using Method 1, make 24 copies of page 45.) Choose 4 pairs of light and dark fabrics.

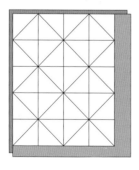

Place **right sides together**.

Each pair makes 40 triangle units.

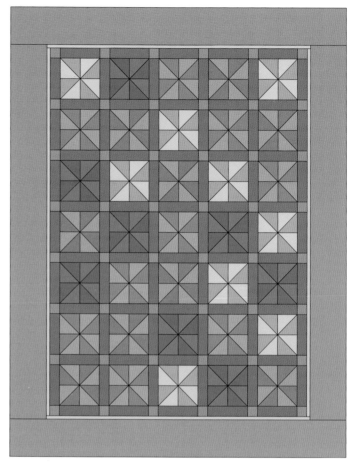

2. BLOCKS: Make 35 blocks as shown. Press.

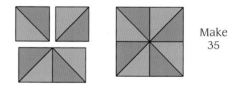

Make 35

3. ASSEMBLY: Arrange blocks and sashing as shown on page 35. Stitch into horizontal rows. Stitch rows together. Press.

4. BORDER 1: Make 2 side borders by piecing strips to same length as quilt. Stitch to quilt. Press. Repeat at top and bottom. Press. More information in General Directions, page 4.

Continued on page 35

MONTICELLO

55 x 73"   9" Block
See other colorations for this quilt on page 36.

YARDAGE

Choose fabric with 42" usable width.
We do not recommend prewashing fat quarters.

Blocks	16 fat quarters - 18" x 21-22"
	8 blue, 8 white
Block centers	½ yd
Border 1	⅜ yd
Border 2	1⅜ yd
Binding	⅝ yd
Backing	3⅝ yd
Batting	61 x 79"

CUTTING

Cut strips selvage to selvage.

Blocks	See Step 1
Block centers	35 squares 3½"
Border 1	8 strips 1" wide
Border 2	8 strips 5" wide
Binding	7 strips 2½" wide

DIRECTIONS

Use ¼" seam allowance unless otherwise noted.

1. BLOCK CUTTING: Choose a method of cutting
   and sewing half-square triangle units from
   General Directions, pages 2-3. This quilt
   requires 3"-finished triangle units. (If using
   Method 1, make 48 copies of page 45.) Choose
   8 pairs of blue and white fabrics and place
   each pair **right sides together**.

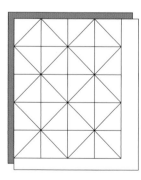

Place **right sides together**.

Each pair makes 40 units.

2. BLOCKS: Make 35 blocks as shown. Press.

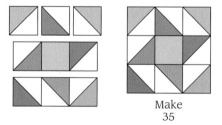

Make
35

3. ASSEMBLY: Arrange blocks as shown on page
   36. Stitch into horizontal rows. Stitch rows
   together. Press.

Continued on page 36

18

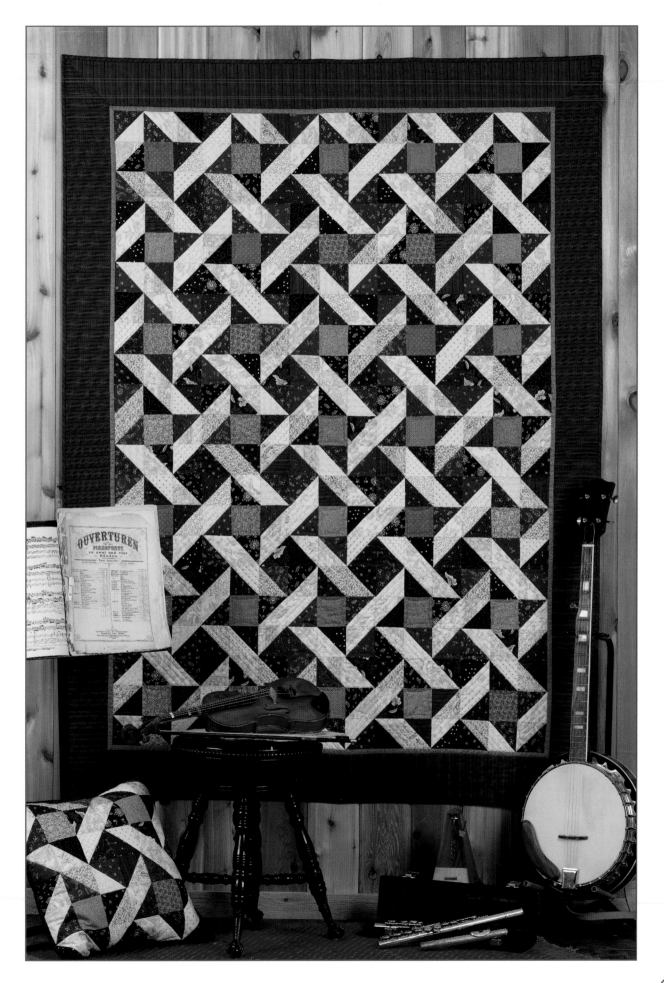

ICE CREAM SOCIAL

60 x 84″   24″ Block

YARDAGE

Choose fabric with 42″ usable width.
We do not recommend prewashing fat quarters.

Blocks,
  binding   16 fat quarters - 18″ x 21-22″
                2 light & 2 dark of blue, green, pink,
                & purple

Border, blocks   3½ yd black
Backing   5⅜ yd
Batting   66 x 90″

CUTTING

Cut strips selvage to selvage.

Blocks   See Step 1
Black   8 strips 6½″ wide - border
          16 pieces 10½ x 15½″ - blocks

DIRECTIONS

Use ¼″ seam allowance unless otherwise noted.

1. BLOCK CUTTING: Choose a method of cutting
   and sewing half-square triangle units from
   General Directions, pages 2-3. Use diagrams to
   cut binding strips, squares, and make triangle
   units. This quilt requires 3″-finished triangle
   units. (If using Method 1, make 32 copies of
   page 45.)

Cut each fat quarter:

 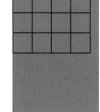

2½ x 21-22″ piece
for binding

12 squares 3½″

Place **right sides
together** with
piece of black.

Each pair makes 12
triangle units.

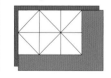

2. BLOCKS: Make 96 units as shown at right. Press.
   Stack units in piles as diagram shows. Make 6
   blocks using 2 units from each pile, rotating
   units as shown. Diagrams continue on page 37.
   Press.

Light squares   Light triangles
Dark triangles   Dark squares

Make 12   Make 12

Make 12   Make 12

Make 12   Make 12

Make 12   Make 12

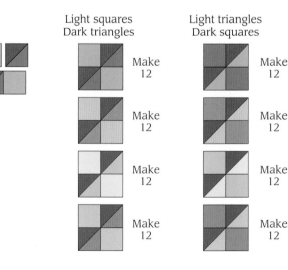

LAVENDER FIELDS

51x51″   12″ Block

YARDAGE

Choose fabric with 42″ usable width.
We do not recommend prewashing fat quarters.

Blocks	8 fat quarters - 18″ x 21-22″
	5 pinks, 3 blues
Border 1	¼ yd
Border 2	⅜ yd
Border 3	1⅛ yd
Binding	⅝ yd
Backing	3½ yd
Batting	57x57″

CUTTING

Cut strips selvage to selvage.

Blocks	See Step 1
Border 1	4 strips 1½″ wide
Border 2	4-5 strips 2″ wide
Border 3	5-6 strips 5½″ wide
Binding	6 strips 2½″ wide

DIRECTIONS

Use ¼″ seam allowance unless otherwise noted.

1. BLOCK CUTTING: Number the pink fabrics 1-5 and the blue fabrics 1-3. Choose a method of cutting and sewing half-square triangle units from General Directions, pages 2-3. Use diagrams to cut squares and make triangle units. This quilt requires 3″-finished triangle units. (If using Method 1, make 10 copies of page 45.)

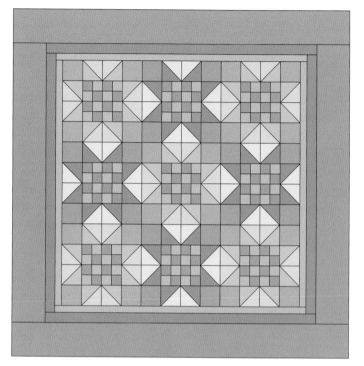

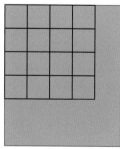

Blue #1
Block B Corners
16 squares 3½″

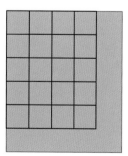

Pink #1
Block A Corners
20 squares 3½″

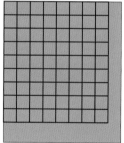

Pink #2
Blocks A&B Centers
72 squares 2″

Pink #3
Blocks A&B Centers
72 squares 2″

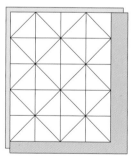

Pink #4 & Blue #2
Block A
Star Point Units
Place **right sides together**
40 triangle units

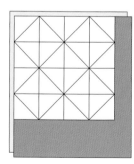

Pink #5 & Blue #3
Block B
Star Point Units
Place **right sides together**
32 triangle units

Continued on page 38

22

HEARTHSIDE HARMONY

65 x 80"   7½" Block
See other colorations for this quilt on page 39.

YARDAGE

Choose fabric with 42" usable width.
We do not recommend prewashing fat quarters.

Blocks   16 fat quarters - 18" x 21-22"
                  8 light, 8 dark

Border 1   ⅝ yd
Border 2   2 yd
Binding   ⅔ yd
Backing   5 yd
Batting   71 x 86"

CUTTING

Cut strips selvage to selvage.

Blocks   See Step 1
Border 1   6 strips 3" wide
Border 2   8 strips 8" wide
Binding   8 strips 2½" wide

DIRECTIONS

Use ¼" seam allowance unless otherwise noted.

1. BLOCK CUTTING: Choose a method of cutting and sewing half-square triangle units from General Directions, pages 2-3. Choose 8 pairs of fabrics, 1 light and 1 dark for each. Use diagrams to cut squares and make triangle units. This quilt requires 2½"-finished triangle units. (If using Method 1, make 16 copies of page 44.)

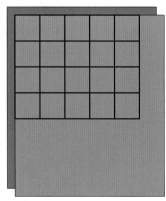

Place pairs **right sides together**.
Cut 20 squares through both layers.
Each pair makes 40 squares.

Keep pairs **right sides together**.
Each pair makes 20 triangle units.

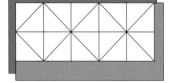

2. BLOCKS: Make 48 blocks as shown creating a light side and a dark side. Press.

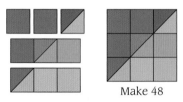

Make 48

3. ASSEMBLY: Arrange blocks as shown in diagram on page 39, rotating light and dark sides to make the design. Stitch into horizontal rows. Stitch rows together. Press.

4. BORDER 1: Make 2 side borders by piecing strips to same length as quilt. Stitch to quilt. Press. Repeat at top and bottom. More information in General Directions, page 4.

5. BORDER 2: Repeat Step 4.

Continued on page 39

24

CARIBBEAN BREEZE

57 x 57"   15" Block
See other colorations for this quilt on page 40.

YARDAGE

Choose fabric with 42" usable width.
We do not recommend prewashing fat quarters.

Blocks   16 fat quarters - 18" x 21-22"
                  4 medium blue, 4 dark blue
                  4 medium green, 4 dark green

Border 1   ⅓ yd
Border 2   1 yd
Binding   ⅝ yd
Backing   3¾ yd
Batting   63 x 63"

CUTTING

Cut strips selvage to selvage.

Blocks   See Step 1
Border 1   5 strips 1½" wide
Border 2   5 strips 5½" wide
Binding   6 strips 2¼" wide

DIRECTIONS

Use ¼" seam allowance unless otherwise noted.

1. BLOCK CUTTING: Choose a method of cutting
   and sewing half-square triangle units from
   General Directions, pages 2-3. This quilt
   requires 2½"-finished triangle units. (If using
   Method 1, make 48 copies of page 44.) Choose
   4 pairs of medium and dark blues. Repeat with
   greens.

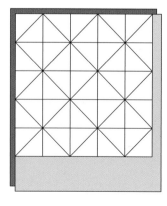
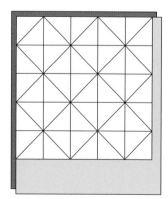

Place **right sides together**.
Each pair makes 50 half-square triangle units.

2. BLOCKS: Make 5 blue blocks and 4 green blocks
   as shown. Press. Make 4 corner blocks with
   remaining green units. Press.

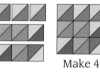
Make 4

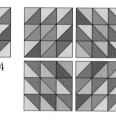
Make 5

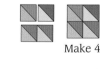

Make 4

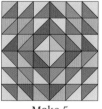
Make 4

3. ASSEMBLY: Arrange blocks as shown on page
   40. Stitch into horizontal rows. Stitch rows
   together. Press.

Continued on page 40

CHELSEA MORNING

58 x 74"   8" Block

YARDAGE

Choose fabric with 42" usable width.
We do not recommend prewashing fat quarters.

Blocks	16 fat quarters - 18" x 21-22" 8 blue, 8 yellow
Border 2, blocks	3 yd white
Applique	⅓ yd each of 2 greens - leaves ½ yd green - vines, tulip leaves
Border 1	⅓ yd
Binding	⅔ yd
Backing	3⅞ yd
Batting	64 x 80"
Fusible web	3 yd

CUTTING

Cut strips selvage to selvage.

White	4 pieces 8½ x 62" - Border 2 cut on lengthwise grain 4 pieces 18" x 21-22"
Blocks	See Step 1
Applique	patterns on page 46 see Step 5 for vine - cut vine fabric 1st 4 tulips & leaves, 4 tulips & leaves reversed 8 circle flowers 4 strips 1¾" wide of each leaf green
Border 1	5 strips 1½" wide
Binding	7-8 strips 2¼" wide

DIRECTIONS

Use ¼" seam allowance unless otherwise noted.

1. BLOCK CUTTING: Choose a method of cutting and sewing half-square triangle units from General Directions, pages 2-3. This quilt requires 2"-finished triangle units. (If using Method 1, make 36 copies of page 43.) Choose fabrics and cut as shown in diagrams.

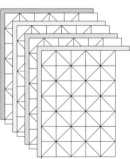

Remaining 4 blues:
Place **right sides together** with white.
Each pair makes 70 triangle units.

Remaining 4 yellows:
Applique

Continued on page 41

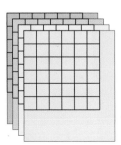

Choose 4 blues:
Cut 36 squares 2½"
of each

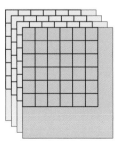

Choose 4 yellows:
Cut 36 squares 2½"
of each

HYDE PARK
Continued from page 6

4. LAYER & QUILT: Piece backing horizontally to same size as batting. Layer, baste, and quilt. Trim batting and backing even with quilt top.

5. BIND: Stitch binding strips together end to end. Press in half lengthwise, wrong sides together. Bind quilt using ⅜″ seam allowance. More information in General Directions, page 5.

3.

OTHER COLORATIONS FOR HYDE PARK

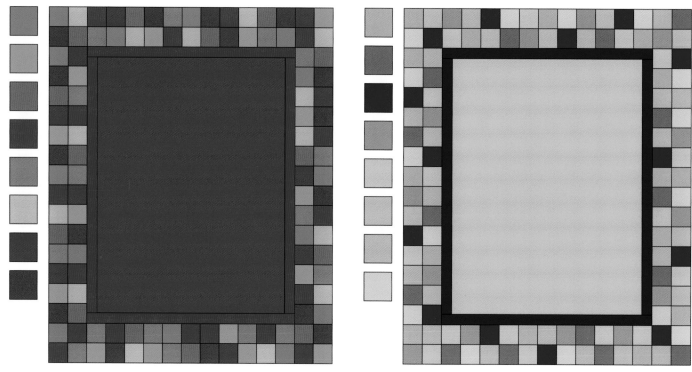

3. BORDER 1: Cut 2 side borders the same length as quilt. Stitch to quilt. Press. Repeat at top and bottom. More information in General Directions, page 4.

4. BORDER 2: Repeat Step 3.

   Mark scallops: Use patterns at right to make plastic or paper templates. Starting at center of side and center of top or bottom, place straight side of template along outer edge of border and mark three scallops toward corner. Use templates to start corner scallop and finish last part of curve by hand. Note that corner scallop is not symmetrical. Repeat for other sides and corners.

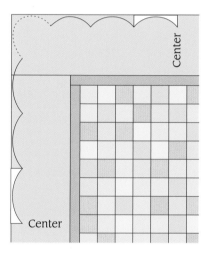

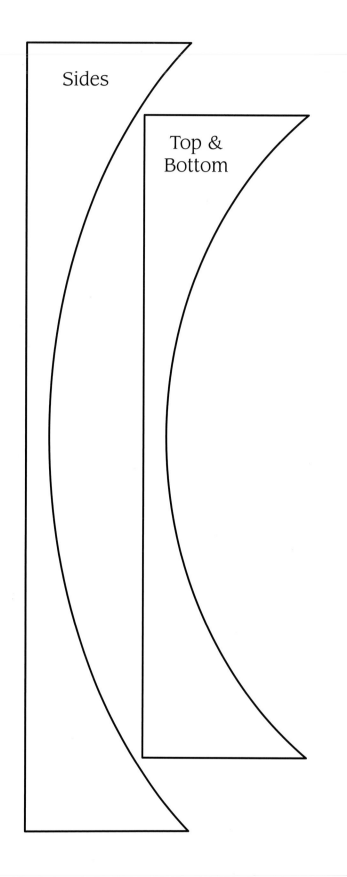

Sides

Top & Bottom

5. LAYER & QUILT: Piece backing horizontally to same size as batting. Layer, baste, and quilt. Echo quilting the scallops is an effective approach for the wide border. To make binding easier, put a line of stitching just inside the marking for the scallops, then trim batting, backing, and quilt top along scallop marking.

6. BIND: For single-fold binding, stitch strips together end to end with diagonal seams. Bind quilt using ⅜" seam allowance, pivoting at inside corners to form miters.

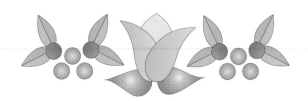

ASHLEY

Continued from page 10

4. BORDER 1: Make 2 side borders by piecing strips to same length as quilt. Stitch to quilt. Press. Repeat at top and bottom. Press. More information in General Directions, page 4.

5. BORDER 2: Repeat Step 4.

6. LAYER & QUILT: Piece backing horizontally to same size as batting. Layer, baste, and quilt. Trim batting and backing even with quilt top.

7. BIND: Stitch binding strips together end to end. Press in half lengthwise, wrong sides together. Bind quilt using ⅜″ seam allowance. More information in General Directions, page 5.

5.

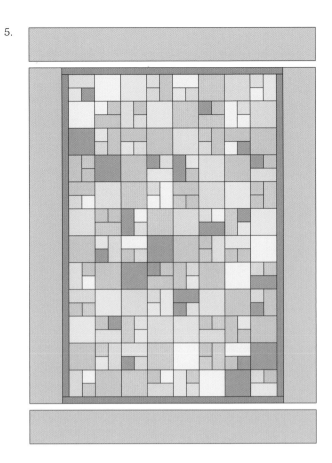

OTHER COLORATIONS FOR ASHLEY

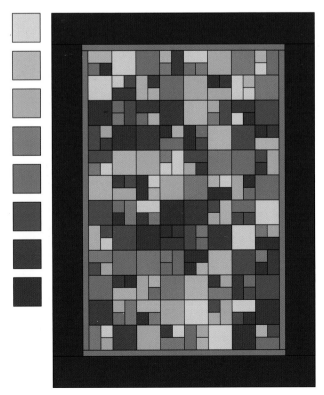

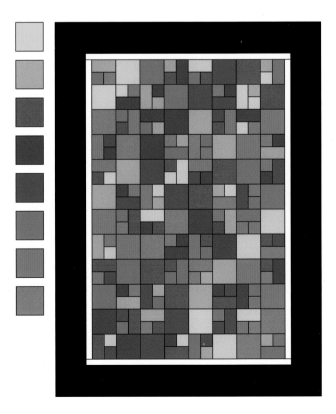

BUTTERFLY KISSES
Continued from page 12

cross corners of blocks. Place plain leaves in sets of 6 between flowers. Place butterflies in centers of blocks as shown. Fuse. Stitch edges using machine blanket stitch or zigzag. Antennae can be quilted, embroidered, or drawn with permanent marker.

5. BORDERS: Refer to General Directions, Borders - Mitered Corner, pages 4-5.

6. LAYER & QUILT: Piece backing horizontally to same size as batting. Layer, baste, and quilt. Trim batting and backing even with quilt top.

7. BIND: Stitch binding strips together end to end. Press in half lengthwise, wrong sides together. Bind quilt using ⅜" seam allowance. More information in General Directions, page 5.

3.

OTHER COLORATIONS FOR BUTTERFLY KISSES

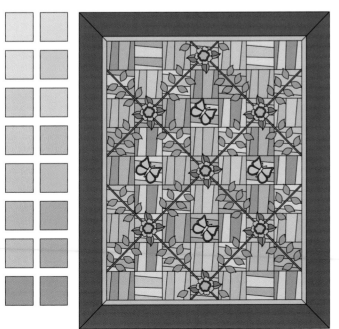

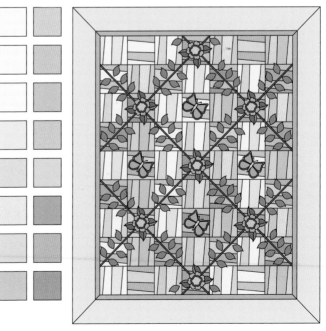

CONFETTI
Continued from page 14

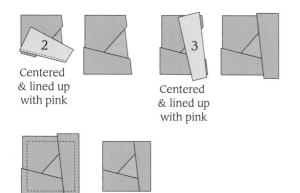

Centered & lined up with pink

Centered & lined up with pink

Trim to 6½″ square

Make 63

3.

3. ASSEMBLY: Arrange blocks in rows as shown, rotating as desired. Stitch into horizontal rows. Stitch rows together. Press.

4. LAYER & QUILT: Piece backing horizontally to same size as batting. Layer, baste, and quilt. Trim batting and backing even with quilt top.

5. BIND: Stitch binding strips together end to end. Press in half lengthwise, wrong sides together. Bind quilt using ⅜″ seam allowance. More information in General Directions, page 5.

OTHER COLORATIONS FOR CONFETTI

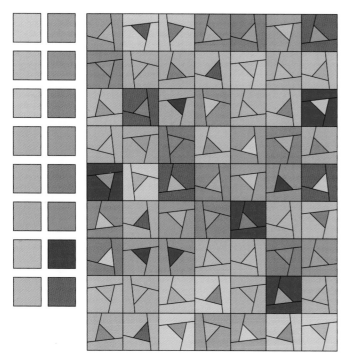

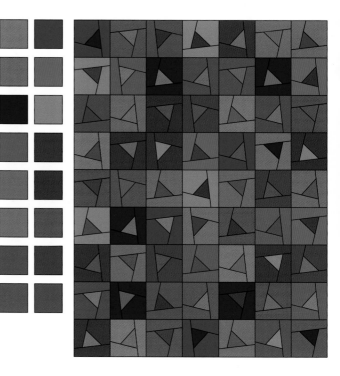

SAFARI
Continued from page 16

5. BORDER 2: Repeat Step 4.

6. LAYER & QUILT: Piece backing horizontally to same size as batting. Layer, baste, and quilt. Trim batting and backing even with quilt top.

7. BIND: Stitch binding strips together end to end. Press in half lengthwise, wrong sides together. Bind quilt using ⅜″ seam allowance. More information in General Directions, page 5.

OTHER COLORATIONS FOR SAFARI

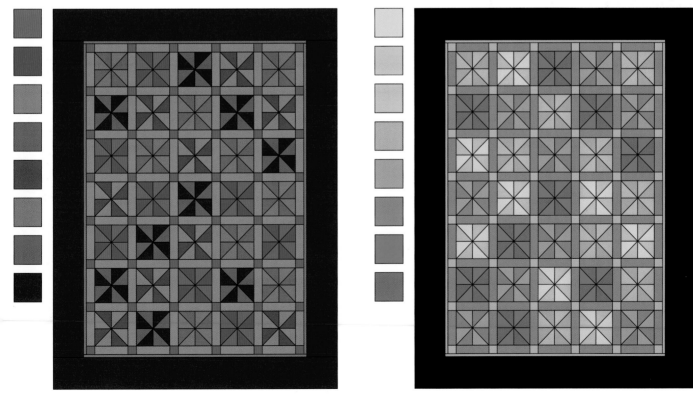

MONTICELLO
Continued from page 18

4. BORDERS: Refer to General Directions, Borders - Mitered Corner, pages 4-5.

5. LAYER & QUILT: Piece backing horizontally to same size as batting. Layer, baste, and quilt. Trim batting and backing even with quilt top.

6. BIND: Stitch binding strips together end to end. Press in half lengthwise, wrong sides together. Bind quilt using ⅜″ seam allowance. More information in General Directions, page 5.

3.

OTHER COLORATIONS FOR MONTICELLO

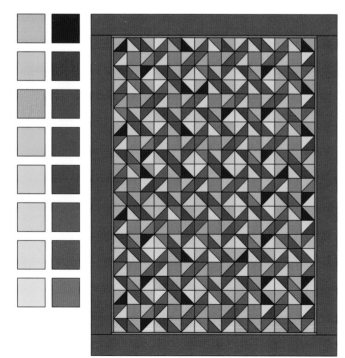

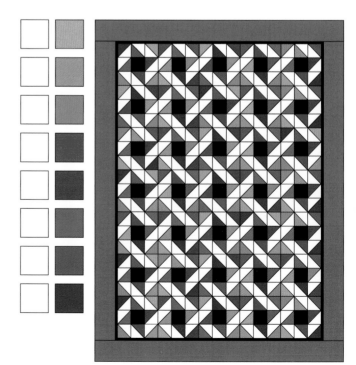

36

ICE CREAM SOCIAL

Continued from page 20

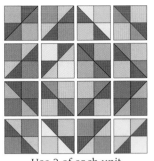 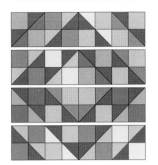

Use 2 of each unit
to make 1 block

Make 6

4. BORDER: Make 2 side borders by piecing strips to same length as quilt. Stitch to quilt. Press. Repeat at top and bottom. More information in General Directions, page 4.

5. LAYER & QUILT: Piece backing vertically to same size as batting. Layer, baste, and quilt. Trim batting and backing even with quilt top.

6. BIND: Stitch binding pieces together end to end, mixing colors randomly. Press in half lengthwise, wrong sides together. Bind quilt using ⅜" seam allowance. More information in General Directions, page 5.

3. ASSEMBLY: Arrange blocks as shown. Stitch into horizontal rows. Stitch rows together. Press.

2. BLOCKS: Make 9 blocks as shown. Press.

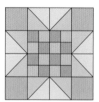

Make
40

Make
20

Make
9

Make
32

Make
16

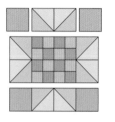

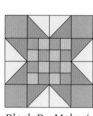

Block A - Make 5

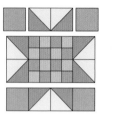

Block B - Make 4

3. ASSEMBLY: Arrange blocks as shown. Stitch into horizontal rows. Stitch rows together. Press.

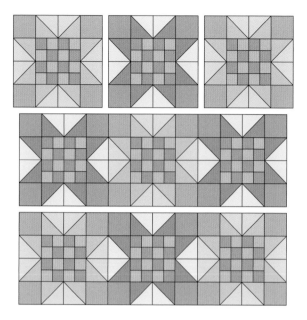

4. BORDER 1: Cut 2 side borders the same length as quilt. Stitch to quilt. Press. Repeat at top and bottom. More information in General Directions, page 4.

5. BORDERS 2 & 3: Repeat Step 4, piecing border strips end to end as needed.

6. LAYER & QUILT: Piece backing to same size as batting. Layer, baste, and quilt. Trim batting and backing even with quilt top.

7. BIND: Stitch binding strips together end to end. Press in half lengthwise, wrong sides together. Bind quilt using ⅜″ seam allowance. More information in General Directions, page 5.

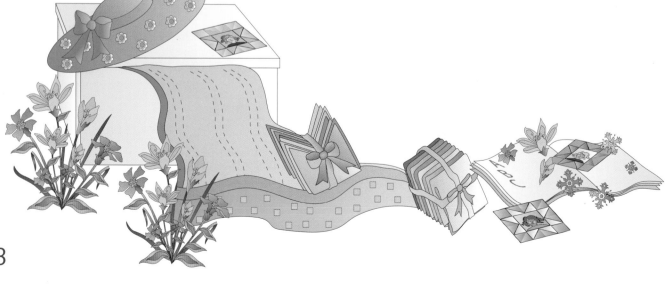

HEARTHSIDE HARMONY
Continued from page 24

6. LAYER & QUILT: Piece backing vertically to same size as batting. Layer, baste, and quilt. Trim batting and backing even with quilt top.

7. BIND: Stitch binding strips together end to end. Press in half lengthwise, wrong sides together. Bind quilt using ⅜″ seam allowance. More information in General Directions, page 5.

3.

OTHER COLORATIONS FOR HEARTHSIDE HARMONY

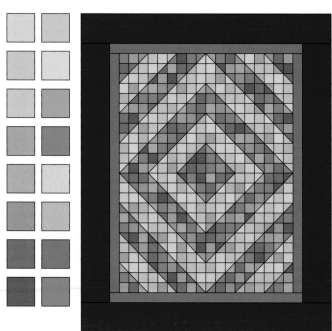

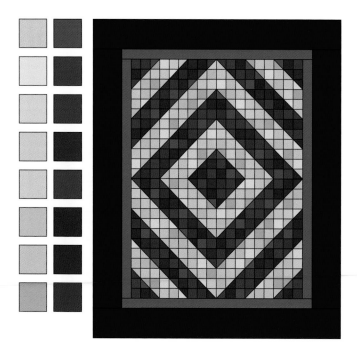

CARIBBEAN BREEZE

Continued from page 26

4. BORDER 1: Make 2 side borders by piecing strips to same length as quilt. Stitch to quilt. Press. Repeat at top and bottom. Press. More information in General Directions, page 4.

5. BORDER 2: Make 4 borders the same length/width as quilt. Stitch two to opposite sides of quilt. Press. Stitch corner blocks to each end of remaining borders, oriented as shown in whole-quilt diagram on page 26. Stitch to top and bottom of quilt. Press.

6. LAYER & QUILT: Piece backing to same size as batting. Layer, baste, and quilt. Trim batting and backing even with quilt top.

7. BIND: Stitch binding strips together end to end. Press in half lengthwise, wrong sides together. Bind quilt using ¼″ seam allowance. More information in General Directions, page 5.

3.

OTHER COLORATIONS FOR CARIBBEAN BREEZE

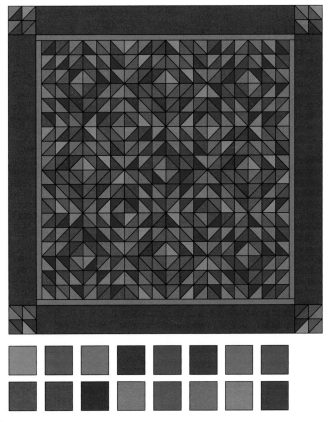

40

CHELSEA MORNING
Continued from page 28

2. BLOCKS: Make 18 yellow and 17 blue blocks as shown. Press.

For each block:

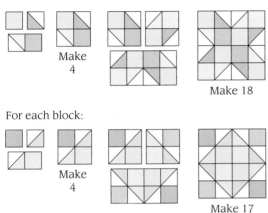

Make 4

Make 18

For each block:

Make 4

Make 17

3. ASSEMBLY: Arrange blocks as shown. Stitch into horizontal rows. Stitch rows together. Press.

4. BORDER 1: Make 2 side borders by piecing strips to same length as quilt. Stitch to quilt. Press. Repeat at top and bottom. Press. More information in General Directions, page 4.

5. BORDER 2 & APPLIQUE:

Find center of each border by folding in half and marking lightly. Borders will be trimmed to exact length after applique is complete.

For vines, fuse web to wrong side of 15x20″ piece of vine fabric. Cut sixteen ½″x 18″ **bias** strips. Remove paper backing and place vines in position, centered on each border and out of seam allowances. Do not fuse yet. Use diagrams and photo as guides.

For leaves, stitch pairs of green strips together lengthwise. Press. Fuse web to wrong side of strip sets. Cut 8 large and 32 small leaves from strip sets. Place flowers and leaves on borders with vines, keeping them out of seam allowances. Fuse. Stitch edges of appliques using machine blanket stitch or zigzag. Trim side borders to fit quilt (center and trim from both ends). Stitch to quilt. Press. Repeat at top and bottom.

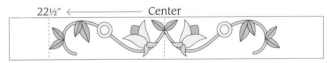

22½″ ← —————— Center

6. LAYER & QUILT: Piece backing horizontally to same size as batting. Layer, baste, and quilt. Trim batting and backing even with quilt top.

7. BIND: Stitch binding strips together end to end. Press in half lengthwise, wrong sides together. Bind quilt using ¼″ seam allowance. More information in General Directions, page 5.

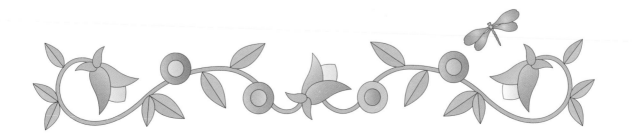

IDEAS FOR LEFTOVER UNITS OR BLOCKS

Make pillows or small wall hangings with your extra squares and units. Add other fabrics and borders as needed to make the desired size and design.

SUNNY DAYS

Add a wide ruffle for a pretty pillow.

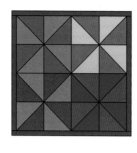

SAFARI

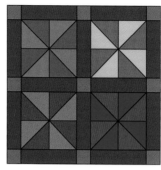

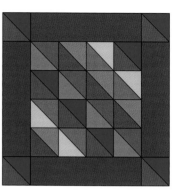

MONTICELLO

CARIBBEAN BREEZE

HEARTHSIDE HARMONY

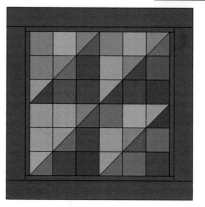

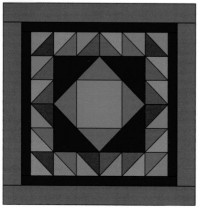

42

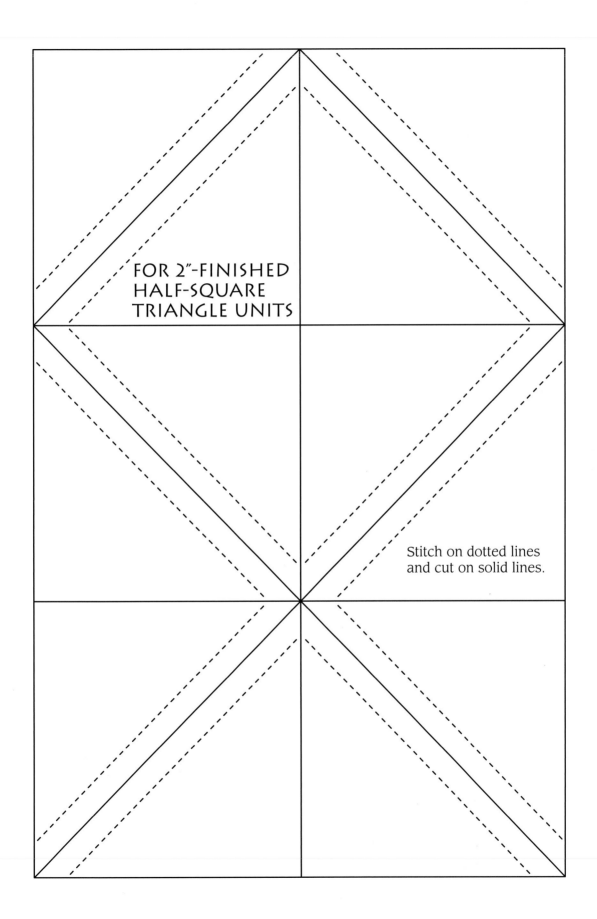

FOR 2"-FINISHED
HALF-SQUARE
TRIANGLE UNITS

Stitch on dotted lines
and cut on solid lines.

Photocopy the required number of pages on a
copier that reproduces at an accurate 100%.

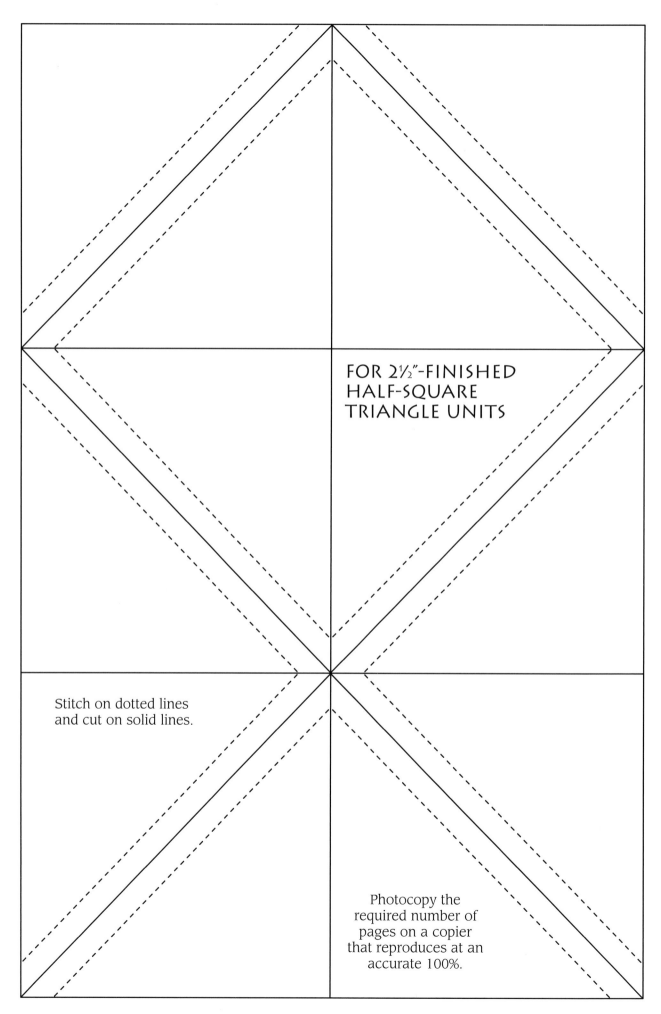

FOR 2½″-FINISHED
HALF-SQUARE
TRIANGLE UNITS

Stitch on dotted lines
and cut on solid lines.

Photocopy the
required number of
pages on a copier
that reproduces at an
accurate 100%.

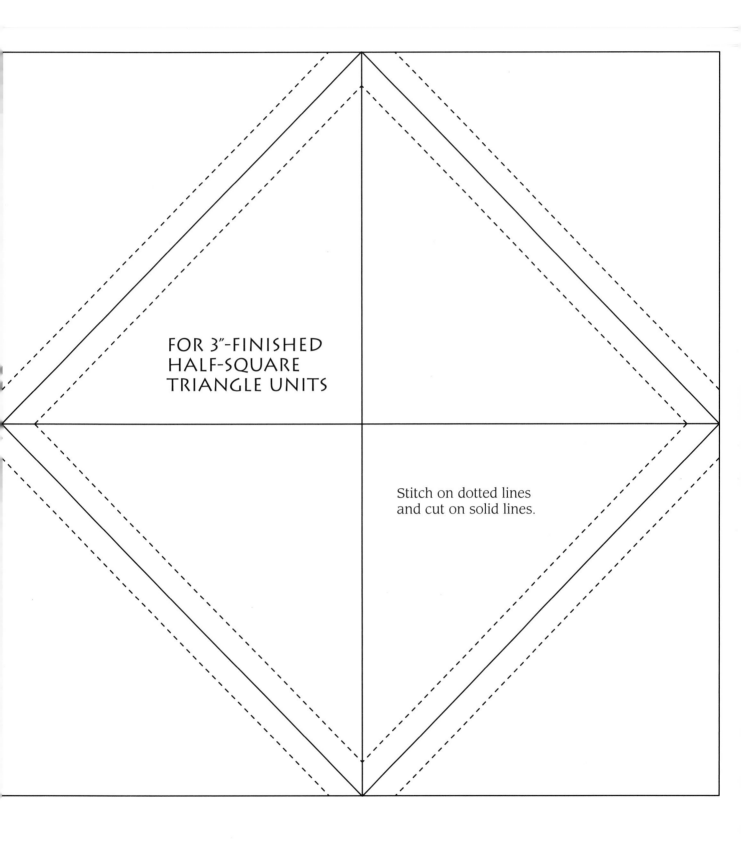

FOR 3"-FINISHED
HALF-SQUARE
TRIANGLE UNITS

Stitch on dotted lines
and cut on solid lines.

CHELSEA
MORNING

46

Patterns are reversed for tracing to fusible web.

BUTTERFLY KISSES

A FEW MORE POSSIBILITIES®

Home for the Harvest
A Collection of Patchwork & Applique

BedWarmers
Comforter Covers, Toppers, Pillows & More!
by Lynda Milligan & Nancy Smith

Comforts of Love
by Lynda Milligan & Nancy Smith

Divide &
Quilt it Your Way

Hearts A Plenty
Lynda Milligan & Nancy Smith

Comforter covers, coordinated toppers, pillow covers, and pillowcases.
$22.95

18 fall quilts and 20 small projects. Themes include back-to-school, Halloween, & Thanksgiving.
$26.95

6 cozy patchwork quilts with coordinating pillow covers to complete the look.
$16.95

17 quilts to assemble using 4 different innovative "divide and conquer" techniques.
$25.95

19 quilt patterns to warm your heart. 8 small bonus projects for you to make and share.
$26.95

Favorite Quilts

Friends FOREVER
Quilting Together

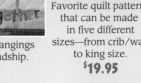

P.S. I LOVE YOU THREE!
by Lynda Milligan & Nancy Smith

Super Simple Squares
Creative Uses for 6½" Squares

WELCOME TO MY CABIN
NANCY SMITH & LYNDA MILLIGAN

20 quilts and wall hangings that celebrate friendship.
$26.95

Favorite quilt patterns that can be made in five different sizes—from crib/wall to king size.
$19.95

21 charming quilts for babies, toddlers, and young children.
$22.95

18 super simple quilts using packets of 6½" squares or strips.
$18.95

Welcome to My Cabin quilt with 13 other projects that use elements taken from the main pattern.
$19.95

TOPPERS 2
Lynda Milligan & Nancy Smith

SUPER SIMPLE STRIPS
NANCY SMITH & LYNDA MILLIGAN

Home for the Holidays
Lynda Milligan & Nancy Smith

RED HOT ATTITUDE
Nancy Smith & Lynda Milligan

15 different quilts to display on beds, couches, or tables.
$21.95

18 fantastic quilts to create from precut 6½" strips or yardage.
$18.95

12 quilts and other projects that will wrap you in warmth and love this holiday season.
$20.95

5 quilted wall hangings and many unique accessories to give your friends.
$16.95

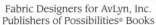

POSSIBILITIES®
Fabric Designers for AvLyn, Inc.
Publishers of Possibilities® Books

Phone 303-740-6206 • Fax 303-220-7424 • Orders only U.S. & Canada 1-800-474-2665 • www.possibilitiesquilt.com